A MOSAIC OF MY CANADIAN NEIGHBOURS

AUTHOR: CHANTAL V. MAGRACIA - OULDZINI   A.K.A.   "SELMA"

EDITOR:	SAM WRIGHT
ILLUSTRATOR:	EMAN ABIDA
FORMATTER:	FAISAL ADEEL / MUHAMMAD BILAL
BOOK PROMO:	SHAINA JAVED

First published in Canada in 2020 by Chantal Magracia.
Copyright © 2020 Chantal Magracia
ISBN: 978 - 1 - 7772044 - 1 - 9

FREE DOWNLOADABLE WORKSHEETS

TEACHERS & PARENTS,
If you would like to access the worksheets for this specific book:
1. Please go to my website: philmorcan.com
2. The worksheets would be under the heading "FREE DOWNLOADS".

philmorcan.com
philmorcan@gmail.com
facebook.com/philmorcan
instagram.com/philmorcan
youtube.com = subscribe to "PhilMorCan"
Amazon.ca = search for "Chantal Magracia"

DEDICATION

I would like to dedicate this gift to my strong, intelligent, independent, brave, courageous, enlightened, and empowered friends who support and fight for the equality, human rights, and freedoms of the oppressed, the needy, the poor, and the vulnerable populations of our global community:

Shirley Tran	Sevda Ciplak	Amanda Pike	Sumaya Yusuf
Afsheen Chak	Firoza Osman	Yashmin Khan	Dr. Tania Nordli
Marcia Lee	Alvina Al-Zaydi	Angel Al-Zaydi	Gyesuk Anna Yang

I would also like to extend my gratitude to my sisters from "The Alberta Society of Islamic Fellowship" (ASIF) for all of their wisdom and support. These are a group of intelligent, capable, and successful mentors and leaders who strengthens me and uplifts me to be better everyday and do more everyday for the community we serve:

Evelyn Serbout	Mary Joe Aissa	Heidi Parel	Suzan Nihad
Jelena Babic	Shabina Khadri	Fathima Khadri	Dr. Shameeza Khan
Maryem Ait Ali	Adila Hamad	Afshan Fatima	Mechil Templado

A PORTION OF THE PROCEEDS OF THIS BOOK IS PLEDGED TO BE DIRECTLY DONATED TO "THE ALBERTA SOCIETY OF ISLAMIC FELLOWSHIP":

The Alberta Society of Islamic Fellowship "ASIF" aims to provide programs, activities, classes/courses, and events for FREE or for a nominal cost, that meets the physical, emotional, moral, and intellectual needs of babies, children, youth, women, men, and elderly personnel of our community, in order to successfully adapt them to the Canadian culture and norms, as well as, the Alberta climate and weather, while keeping our Islamic beliefs, values, and principles intact. In this way, we help foster healthy Islamic family and communal relationships, networks, and support systems. If you'd like to donate to their mission, vision, goals, & causes, you may do so at:

treasurer.asif@gmail.com

Live, Laugh, Love, & Light,
Chantal V. Magracia - Ouldzini a.k.a. "Selma"

A Mosaic Of My Canadian Neighbours 4

You know, I grew up in Canada, but I wasn't born here. My parents are not from here either. My mom is from the Philippines and my dad is from Morocco. Somewhere somewhen, they met, got married, had me, immigrated to Canada, bought a house, and invested in several businesses.

For as long as I can remember, Canada's always been my first home. I grew up here. I've made friends here who treat us as their own family and their own blood. We've built our lives here from the ground up.

Every single time we travel somewhere in the world, I always miss the things that I've always been used to, here in Canada:

a clean drinkable water straight from the faucet that doesn't give me diarrhea,

a closed roof above our heads where the lizards, cockroaches, rats, centipedes, and other creepy crawlies cannot invade my living space,

a proper flushing toilet that doesn't clog up and stink up the whole house,

a trustworthy vehicle that doesn't break in the middle of the highway to bring us to and from places.

I never knew how important easy access to these things were until I visited places that didn't readily have these available at my disposal.

I have the personality of a cowboy. I'm flexible. I'm easygoing. I'm personable. I'm agreeable. I always smile and laugh often. I don't complain much, if at all. I go with the flow. I'm a "YES" person. So, please don't think that I'm looking down on others or making fun of their circumstances -- that is not my intention, not at all. Honestly, I have so much respect for different people, cultures, religions, norms, way of thinking, and way of life.

Rather, the list above simply refers to the things I miss the most when I'm not in Canada. This is why I've always felt that Canada is my true home because I feel more comfortable here, I feel safer here, and I feel more secure here. If something happened to me or my parents, I'd know exactly what to do or who to contact.

My parents and I are extremely close because I'm their only daughter, so not only am I their most favourite child because they have no other choice, but I'm also the recipient of all their love, attention, and affection. I guess anyone can say I have it good, although sometimes, it can get quite lonely when they're both extremely busy with work because someone's got to pay for the house, the food, the car, the clothes, and the gadgets, right? But hey, I make this time my "ME TIME".

Most recently, my parents, Latifa and Mustafa Fsahi, gave me a tablet for my 12th birthday.

"Nanay and Abi, you both know that you didn't have to get me something this fancy, right?" The Tagalog term 'Nanay' means mother, while the Arabic term 'Abi' means father.

"I know, anak, but nowadays, you get so much homework that is research-based and I thought it would be nice for you to have your own gadget to do that with, and not have to wait for me to finish my work before you can do yours." The Tagalog term 'anak' means child.

"Thank you so much po, Nanay and Abi. I'm truly and deeply grateful for your gift. It's beautiful, but I just didn't want you to have to spend money on me, especially when the economy is this bad." We must add the word "po" somewhere in the conversation to show anyone older than us or anyone with authority that we respect them.

"That's for your dad and I to worry about, anak. You shouldn't have to worry about the economy at your age. Just focus on your schoolwork and that would make me the happiest!"

* MR. & MRS. CORDOVA - RAYNER *

Then, suddenly, the doorbell rang, which startled everyone because we usually never have visitors in our house. Who could it possibly be? I was so excited that I sprang from my chair and ran for the door as quickly as I could. My parents followed after me.

I was taken aback to find Mr. and Mrs. Cordova - Rayner at our doorstep. Usually, I only see them from afar -- gardening, mowing, snowblowing, and lounging in their front yard. Basically, they have a lot of time on their hands because they're both retired veterans now.

My parents always taught me that a smile is a form of charity, so I gave them my widest smile, "Hello, Mr. and Mrs. Cordova - Rayner! To what do we owe this pleasure?"

"Oh, Angelica, you are always as cheery as we remember you! Well, Mr. Cordova - Rayner and I just came over to personally ask you if you wanted to have our huge 'National Geographic' collection that's just been collecting dust since the 1980's and because we've invested so much of our money into it, we would like to give it to someone who deserves it, someone who cares, and someone who reads, and we thought of you! Your parents have mentioned in a happenstance that you love maps, love history, and love culture -- well, these magazines are exactly that!"

A Mosaic Of My Canadian Neighbours 8

I nodded profusely with the biggest smile on my face that my cheeks hurt. I could NOT believe my luck! I stood there, frozen, as if time stood still … still gathering my thoughts and my composure. What just happened? I just couldn't fathom that out of everyone they know, they chose me to inherit their leather-bound magazine collection of 40 years' worth of material! I do not know anyone who is luckier than me, happier than me, more blessed than me, and more grateful than me at THIS VERY MOMENT but me, myself, and I. Does that even make sense?

Mr. Cordova - Rayner then interjected, "Of course, I'm a proud collector myself and I know that I've taken very good care of my collection and you will see once you get your hands on them that all of them are still in great, mint condition. Being a perfectionist, I never give anything away in less than perfect condition."

"I don't doubt you, Mr. Cordova - Rayner! I've seen how conscientious you are and how much of a perfectionist you are -- your lush and perfectly manicured garden is enough proof of that because anything that blooms so well is obviously showered with a lot of love, a lot of attention, and a lot of time. From the very bottom of my heart, thank you very much for choosing me to inherit your most prized possession. I can't even begin to comprehend how lucky and blessed I am to be your chosen recipient. I am forever grateful."

"Oh, you're quite welcome, young lady! We're just happy that our collection is going to a good home. We know how much you love reading. We always see you with your head stuck in a book, dear."

"Oh, Mrs. Cordova - Rayner, that is extremely generous of you and Mr. Cordova - Rayner. Would you both like to come in and have some Moroccan mint tea with us? My dad just finished making a fresh batch, and my mom just took out her infamous roasted chicken from the oven!"

My parents seconded, "We insist."

"That's really kind of your family, Angelica. Of course, we'd love to, if you insist. We have never turned down any sumptuous and scrumptious food and beverages ever."

It turned out to be a lovely afternoon brunch with Mr. and Mrs. Cordova - Rayner in our house. My parents always taught me to show a lot of respect for the elderly because the elderly have done a lot for our great nation. I mean, they're the ones who built our nation from the ground up, right? That deserves a mountain of respect! My parents told me that the elderly simply need people to talk to and the elderly simply need to be listened to -- it makes them the happiest to have companions who listens.

I love spending time with the elderly. They've lived so long that they are the most interesting story-tellers -- they not only have a lot of opinions, but they also have a lot of wisdom to share. Honestly, I learn so much simply by listening to their stories about what happened to them and how they overcame their adversities and their adversaries. The elderly are truly the world's living treasures, like a living, walking, talking book full of surprises, full of adventures, full of mysteries, and full of knowledge.

In exchange for all the stories and all the knowledge, I do what I can to help Mr. and Mrs. Cordova - Rayner whenever I can. Whenever I see them out and about, I go over and ask them if they need any kind of help.

Even if they're still strong and fast for their age, I still make myself available when they do need help. It's the least that I can do for them! They remind me so much of my grandma whom I call 'Sitti Fatima'. She's Moroccan so she only knows how to speak Arabic and French, and her English is limited. My Sitti Fatima lives with us for 6 months of the year when the weather here in Alberta, Canada is warm enough, but when it gets cold or chilly, she goes back to Morocco, and stays there for 6 months to enjoy the hot weather.

I guess that's one reason why I like to help out the Cordova - Rayners because they remind me so much of my Moroccan grandma and it feels like I'm helping my grandma by helping the Cordova - Rayners. What do they have in common? Strength and speed!

It's been two weeks since my parents gave me a tablet. Since then, I've been using it productively by being updated on current events. Truthfully, I feel a tad bit disheartened and dejected from the news on TV and the news online which puts Muslims in a bad light, as though we're all who they say we are, as though we're one and the same.

But I mean, come on! There are 1.8 billion Muslims in the world! I'm beginning to worry and wonder what others might think of us simply because of how the news portrays us in the media. I'm a Muslim who watches and reads the news on TV and on social media and I feel attacked, disrespected, and rejected in their "US VS. THEM" narrative in the way that they propagate the bad reputation and the bad deeds of other Muslims in an all-encompassing way, as though what other Muslims have done is also my fault, just because I'm a Muslim too! That doesn't even make any sense! The news is supposed to be objective but why have they become so subjective? Pointing fingers, blaming, accusing. W-H-A-T?!

My parents have always told me that, "Islam should not be judged by what any Muslim does because no Muslim is perfect, but Muslims should be judged based on what Islam teaches."

"Asians are <u>NOT</u> a virus!"

"Hispanics are <u>NOT</u> illegal!"

"Black People are <u>NOT</u> threats!"

"Muslims are <u>NOT</u> terrorists!"

"Native Americans are <u>NOT</u> savages!"

According to the "Clear Quran" which is the holy book of the Muslims, translated by Dr. Mustafa Khattab:

"Life is sacred in Islam. The Quran (5:32) states, 'Whoever takes a life, it will be as if they killed all of humanity; and whoever saves a life, it will be as if they saved all of humanity.' Those who manipulate verses from the Quran by taking them out of context to justify violence against innocents contradict the Quran's call for tolerance and peaceful co-existence. Islam is unequivocally against terrorism (see 5:33).

Islam never condones any acts of violence against the innocents, women, children, the elderly, and those retreating in their places of worship. Muslims are not allowed to cut down trees or kill animals.

But even though I feel disheartened and dejected does not make me hopeless. Instead, I remain hopeful. Hopeful that even though the news and social media have skewed their portrayal of Muslims one way -- their only way or the highway, I look at Mr. and Mrs. Cordova - Rayner and how they treat my family: how truly kind, how immensely generous, and how genuinely caring they are towards us, and vice versa. I doubt there is anything that the news or social media or trolls on social media can say or do to ruin our good name, our good reputation, our good conversations, or even our good relations with the Cordova - Rayners, or anyone that matters.

Honestly, although our identity is Filipino-Moroccan, and both my mom and I are also Hijabi Muslims, WE ARE CANADIAN. I feel that mostly, we hold the same beliefs, values, and principles as other Canadians around us, which is why my family finds it bizarre the kinds of accusations that we get when some people define what they think Muslims are, who they think Muslims are, and what they assume Muslims should be and project their self-serving thoughts and unintelligible opinions onto peaceful people like my family. Sometimes it hurts, you know? But my parents have always reminded me to keep my head up, smile and laugh often, and prove people wrong through substantial kindness, generosity, and understanding.

I can't ever forget what my dad once told me, "Angelica, I want you to always remember that we should never pay any attention to anyone or anything that is untrue. We only focus on positive people and positive things. We give energy only on things that we can change and the things that we can control. We must use our time productively and wisely on anything and everything that is meaningful and purposeful -- that's how we grow spiritually, emotionally, mentally, and psychologically. What's in our hearts and our pure intentions towards everyone and everything are what matters the most! It's how we make other people feel that is the most important because people will never forget how we made them feel!"

We may be Muslim, and we may speak 4 languages in our home, including English, French, Arabic, and Tagalog, but we're also Canadian. When a tragedy befalls Canada and Canadians, we're as equally devastated as any other Canadian. We feel your pains. We celebrate your triumphs. We pay taxes. We enjoy the Rocky Mountains. We like soccer. We love stand-up comedians. We shovel the snow. We mow the grass. We feel the excruciating and numbing pain of a -40 degrees Celsius weather in Edmonton, Alberta.

Why?
Because like you,
WE ARE CANADIANS TOO.
Anything and everything that affects Canada affects each and every single one of us too:
WE ARE ALL IN THIS TOGETHER.

CANADIAN CHARTER OF RIGHTS, FREEDOMS, & RESPONSIBILITIES

REFERENCE

The **Canadian Charter of Rights and Freedoms** was enacted in 1984. The 1984 Charter enhances the protections provided to Canadians by increasing the number and the extent of our rights and freedoms. In addition, the Charter now forms part of our CONSTITUTION, making it difficult for future governments to decrease or limit the rights and freedoms we currently enjoy. It applies when the government tries to infringe upon the rights of Canadians. However, rights and freedoms are NOT WITHOUT limits. Sometimes, they have to be limited in order to protect the rights and freedoms of others because freedoms are guaranteed only to such reasonable limits as can be justified in a free and democratic society.

MY FUNDAMENTAL FREEDOMS AS A CANADIAN:
1. FREEDOM OF CONSCIENCE & RELIGION.
2. FREEDOM OF THOUGHT, BELIEF, & EXPRESSION.
3. FREEDOM OF ASSOCIATION.

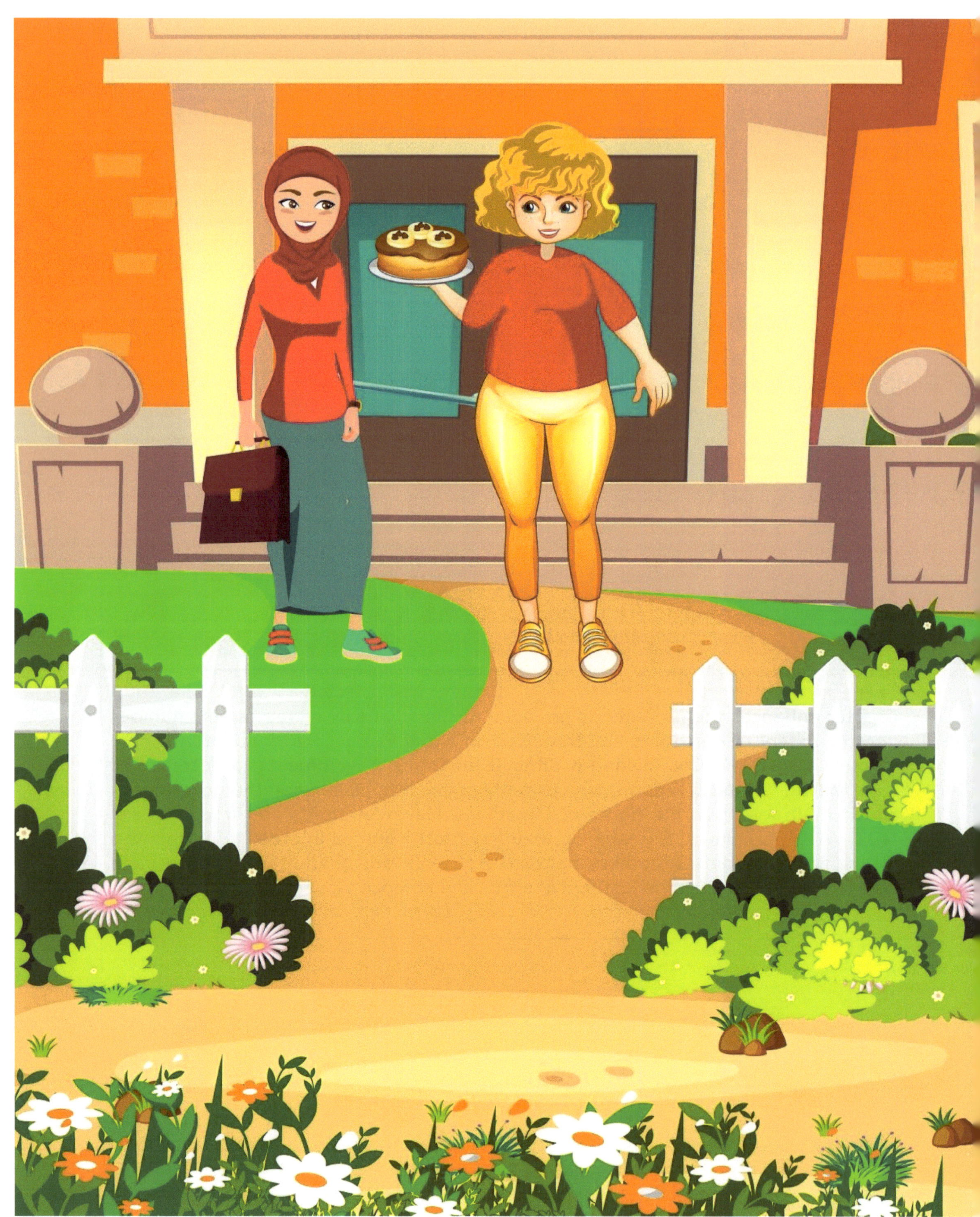

A Mosaic Of My Canadian Neighbours 16

I was walking home after school one day when I saw a glimpse of a woman's silhouette at our front doorstep, so I walked faster to get home.

By the time I reached the door, I was greeted with a very fragrant smell of bananas.

"Hey Angelica, I baked a few dozen banana breads with chocolate chips for a non-profit charity event, and there are a few extras. I figured I'd give some away to my neighbours."

I gave her the biggest hug, "Oh, Mrs. Gaspang - Bidlock, you are the sweetest! I'm starving!" I took the banana bread with chocolate chips off of her hands and said, "How extremely lucky are we? That our neighbour just happens to be a pastry chef? Like seriously, Mrs. Gaspang - Bidlock, thank you, thank you, thank you! You are heaven sent!"

"Don't worry about it, Angelica! I'm just grateful to you, sweetheart, for always taking care of my twins whenever I'm busy with cake orders, and you're always willing to help me out anytime. I truly appreciate that about you. You help without expecting anything in return, and honestly, this is the least that I can do for you. I hope you like it as usual!"

"No worries! I love your twins, Mrs. Gaspang - Bidlock! They're simply too adorable for words, they make me happy, and they keep me company, especially when I get really bored with being an only child and all. Also, you know how much I love everything you make, don't you? Maybe I'll even be a pastry chef like you someday!"

"Well, follow your heart, sweet tooth! I meant, follow your heart, sweetheart! Or, in this case, follow your taste buds! Anyways, I've got to go to the event with the twins now. I wouldn't want to be late considering it's for charity. I'll come by again later with more treats, ok? Or if you want, you can even come by tomorrow because I'm teaching the twins how to make macarons. I'll teach you too, so come over tomorrow afternoon, and we'll make the best tasting macarons ever! You're going to love it, I'm sure!" Mrs. Gaspang - Bidlock left with a huge smile on her face. She's a person that makes you feel light, as light as a cloud, with a trail of rainbows and cakes behind her, around her, in front of her ... everywhere. Honestly, she's one of the most thoughtful people I know.

Of course, I'm going to come! I'd be crazy not to! Macarons are my most favourite cookies in the whole entire universe!

* MR. & MRS. BARRETTO - FSAHI *

My mom is Filipino and her name is Angelina Barretto on official documents but people know her as Dr. Latifa Fsahi -- 'Latifa' means 'gentle' or 'pleasant' because she had requested my Moroccan grandmother to give her a Muslim name. Of course, it was optional but it was her choice. My dad is Moroccan and his name is Mustafa Fsahi. I am a Filipino-Moroccan-Canadian and I am also a Hijabi Muslim, and in reality, not everyone is as bad as the news or social media makes us seem. We have the most wonderful and the most amazing Canadian neighbours who not only tolerate us but who actually accept us, understand us, and respect us exactly for who we are as people. What I love about my Canadian neighbours is that they take the time to get to know us -- who we are and what we're about. They don't judge us by our hijabs or our skin colour, you know? I deeply appreciate that about Canadians.

You know what else I appreciate? I appreciate being in Canada and being a Canadian myself. In Canada, the government encourages us to be a mosaic instead of a melting pot because Canadians recognize and understand that there is strength and power in diversity, and Canadians understand that everyone from all over the world brings unique skill sets from their unique backgrounds which makes Canada a stronger country. Canada respects everyone from all backgrounds and from all walks of life, and accepts that we're all different in beautiful ways and our differences also make us as amazing as we are now.

Canada doesn't force everyone to be one and the same, instead, Canadians capitalize on our differences. Canada recognizes everyone's uniqueness and they nurture it. I saw it happen with my own parents. The Canadian government helped my parents financially by funding their English language classes and their post-secondary upgrading. My mom, who's from the Philippines, spoke Tagalog as her first language and English as her second language, so she only needed to upgrade some courses to be able to practice her profession. My mom is a professor, Dr. Angelina (Latifa) Barretto - Fsahi. But my dad had to attend English language classes first because his first language is Arabic, his second language is French, and his third language is English. My dad, Mustafa Fsahi, is a heavy equipment operator. The most important thing was that the Canadian government was supportive in helping my parents get settled well in this great nation. Afterwards, once my parents got settled finally, then, they had to pay the Canadian government back, so that the Canadian government can continue to help others migrating and immigrating to Canada as newcomers as well. They are happy to pay back the Government of Canada quickly, especially when they know that the Canadian government has myriad programs in place that help the vulnerable, the poor, the needy, and the newcomers. My parents love the idea that Canadians take care of each other, you know?

CANADIAN CHARTER OF RIGHTS, FREEDOMS, & RESPONSIBILITIES

REFERENCE

MY CANADIAN CITIZENSHIP RESPONSIBILITIES:

4.   TAKING RESPONSIBILITY FOR ONESELF AND ONE'S FAMILY:
GETTING A JOB, TAKING CARE OF ONE'S FAMILY AND WORKING HARD IN KEEPING WITH ONE'S ABILITIES ARE IMPORTANT CANADIAN VALUES. WORK CONTRIBUTES TO PERSONAL DIGNITY AND SELF-RESPECT, AND TO CANADA'S PROSPERITY.

GREAT CONDITION CLOTHES
GREAT CONDITION CLOTHES
GREAT CONDITION CLOTHES

* MR. & MRS. LINTAG - BO LASSEN *

Of course, we have other neighbours who prefer to be anonymous and give or donate anonymously; however, thanks to our doorbell camera, we know every single person who comes to our front yard, front doorstep, backyard, and back doorstep.

Mrs. Lintag Bo - Lassen: she's MY Social Studies teacher to be exact, and it's because of her that I've been obsessed with Japan, the Japanese culture, the Japanese language, and Japanese food. She has a way of making us fall in love with her subject. I'm in love with the whole idea of the shoguns and the samurais.

Anyways, Mrs. Lintag Bo - Lassen always leaves used clothes on our doorstep. She has three daughters who are all older than me and whatever clothes they have outgrown, Mrs. Lintag Bo - Lassen gives them to me. She makes sure that she only gives me the ones that are still in great usable condition.

My parents and I appreciate this about Mrs. Lintag Bo - Lassen. We have expressed to her countless times how much money she saves us. For me, as long as I get to save money, and I get to save my parents some money, I am happy. I don't care about clothes too much. I do care about saving money, though. The less money goes out of our pockets, the happier we are as a family because it means we get to use that money for something that actually matters -- something more memorable, unforgettable, and valuable like experiences, travels, adventures, courses, and food.

Mrs. Lintag Bo - Lassen has done this for us not once, not twice, but thrice at this point. Each time, she leaves boxes upon boxes upon boxes of gently used clothing on our doorstep. Each time, she wanted to donate anonymously. Each time, she gets surprised that we figure out that it's her, all thanks to our doorbell camera. In return, we always make couscous with chicken and vegetables for her family because couscous is filling, healthy, and delicious. My mom always says, "We must always take care of the people that care for us and ensure that we only give them the best and the healthiest!"

My parents have always said that we are extremely lucky and blessed to be surrounded by such selfless, thoughtful, and generous people. When we are good to others, the universe also surrounds us with goodness. Not everyone who comes along will be good to us because we can't expect others to be good to us just because we are good to them. However, we mostly attract positive people with a growth mindset around us because we attract to ourselves the same like-minded people.

After school, my mom and I baked our favourite chocolate cake and brought it over to Mrs. Lintag Bo - Lassen's house. I rang the doorbell and Mrs. Lintag Bo - Lassen greeted us at the door with a huge smile on her face, "Hello Angelica and Dr. Fsahi!"

With a huge smile on my face, I said, "Hello, Mrs. Lintag Bo - Lassen!"

My mom said, "Hello, Mrs. Lintag Bo - Lassen, we just came by to give you our freshly baked chocolate cake to thank you for the boxes of clothes that you left on our front porch again. From the bottom of our hearts, we truly can't even thank you enough for your thoughtfulness and generosity."

Mrs. Lintag Bo - Lassen replied, "Oh, don't mind it! I prefer to give them to someone I know, especially to Angelica, because she's one of my highly motivated and extremely studious students! I love having her in my class. I wouldn't be surprised if she became the first woman Prime Minister of Canada, you know? Don't forget me when that happens, dear. It's only a matter of time now -- a question of when. I'm just happy that I can give them away to someone who deserves them. Save your money for college tuition, ok?"

"Absolutely, Mrs. Lintag Bo - Lassen! Who wouldn't want to be the first woman Prime Minister of Canada? That would be super amazing! If I do become one, I will follow the footsteps of Jacinda Ardern, the Prime Minister of New Zealand, because she's doing a phenomenal job running her country. I can only aspire to become like her someday."

"You can be anything you want to be, Angelica! I mean, you can even be a princess if you put your mind to it. Meghan Markle became a princess. I'm sure you can be one too, Angelica -- someone who is as intelligent and kind-hearted as you deserve to be a woman of great influence and great power someday . . . like a Princess or a Prime Minister."

"I think I'll stick to being the first woman Prime Minister of Canada, Mrs. Lintag Bo - Lassen! Thank you for thinking so highly of me, though. You're the best teacher ever! Thank you so much for always encouraging me to be the best version of myself. I've never met such an amazing teacher until I met you! I love you so much!" I gave her the tightest embrace.

Then, Mrs. Lintag Bo - Lassen opened the door fully to let us into her house, so we could eat the cake together.

CANADIAN CHARTER OF RIGHTS, FREEDOMS, & RESPONSIBILITIES

REFERENCE

MY DEMOCRATIC RIGHTS AS A CANADIAN:
5.   EVERY ADULT CANADIAN CITIZEN HAS THE RIGHT TO VOTE.
6.   EVERY ADULT CANADIAN CITIZEN HAS THE RIGHT TO RUN FOR PUBLIC OFFICE.
7.   ELECTIONS, BOTH FEDERAL & PROVINCIAL, MUST BE CALLED EVERY 5 YEARS.
8.   PARLIAMENT & LEGISLATURES MUST SIT TOGETHER AT LEAST ONCE EVERY 12 MONTHS.

MY CITIZENSHIP RESPONSIBILITIES AS A CANADIAN:
9.   VOTING IN ELECTIONS:
THE RIGHT TO VOTE COMES WITH A RESPONSIBILITY TO VOTE IN FEDERAL, PROVINCIAL, OR TERRITORIAL AND LOCAL ELECTIONS.

FILIPINO
CONVENIENCE
STORE
Cookie Duo

✳ MRS. HEIDI PAREL ✳

Our other neighbour, Heidi Parel, is a Muslim Filipino-Canadian, who recently became the new owner of a Filipino grocery store. Whenever we need any Filipino snacks, we always buy them from her store because she sells the tastiest snacks!

Being our neighbour, she also gives us a lot of free food and a lot of discounts. Who wouldn't love going in and out of her store when she gives so much away to others just to make everyone happy when they leave her store? She's such a positive and giving person who is extremely honest about her business transactions that her customers also give her a lot of free stuff in return.

My mom says, "Heidi, I'm sorry, but we can't keep accepting your gifts. These are your products to sell. This is your business and how you feed and take care of your family. It makes me feel bad to keep accepting gifts from you, when you could be selling them to someone else for a good price. You should allow me to pay for these."

"Dr. Fsahi, I don't mind it at all because I don't lose anything by giving. I mean, God blesses us ten-fold when we give what we can to others. God made generosity the greatest moral value. Whenever we give, we get a lot of good karma and a whole lot of blessings from our good deeds. Besides, I know you share a lot of home-made food with your neighbours, and I just want to extend a helping hand by giving you more ingredients to do that with. They say that good food brings people together and nourishes the soul. You cook really well and in my own way, I'm just happy that I'm able to help you in bringing people together and allowing them to experience the greatness of Filipino cuisine through your hands with your delicious home-made meals. Keep doing what you're doing for the community and I'll keep doing my part too."

I thought about it and Mrs. Parel is right. Once a week, my mom cooks a lot of Filipino food to share with our amazing neighbours because it's how she shows she cares for them and that she loves them as people. When my mom likes people, she cooks for them and shares with them her sumptuous and scrumptious Filipino food. Now, I understand why Mrs. Parel always gives us more than what we pay for.

"Well, thank you, Heidi. I truly appreciate everything that you do for my family and our community. I can't thank you enough."

It feels so good to be surrounded by such pure, kind-hearted, and generous souls. What's even more amazing is Mrs. Parel is exactly this kind and generous to everyone she meets in her store regardless of race, religion, language, and culture. She treats everyone exactly the same.

CANADIAN CHARTER OF RIGHTS, FREEDOMS, & RESPONSIBILITIES

REFERENCE

MY CANADIAN CITIZENSHIP RESPONSIBILITIES:
10. HELPING OTHERS IN THE COMMUNITY:
MILLIONS OF VOLUNTEERS FREELY DONATE THEIR TIME TO HELP OTHERS WITHOUT PAY -- HELPING PEOPLE IN NEED, ASSISTING AT YOUR CHILD'S SCHOOL, VOLUNTEERING AT A FOOD BANK OR OTHER CHARITY, OR ENCOURAGING NEWCOMERS TO INTEGRATE. VOLUNTEERING IS AN EXCELLENT WAY TO GAIN USEFUL SKILLS AND DEVELOP FRIENDS AND CONTACTS.

* MRS. SUZAN NIHAD *

Then, there's Mrs. Suzan Nihad, my Iraqi-Canadian teacher, who lives across the street from me. She tutors me Quranic Arabic for free, as long as I pay for her Quranic Arabic curriculum books, which took her 4 years to build and create! Nowadays, is there anyone who would take the time out of their busy lives to tutor others for free? I can't even imagine it! She tutors me twice a week: every Tuesday and every Thursday.

During class one day, I asked my teacher, "Teacher Suzan, why do you give so much of your time and so much of yourself to others? Don't you feel exhausted?"

"Truthfully, I don't feel exhausted at all. Never. I feel happy when I donate my services and my time to others. Do you know why?"

"I would like to know why."

"It's because the most beautiful thing that we can ever give another human being is our time. Do you know why?"

Angelica replies, "Because time is money?"

"No, Angelica. Time is more valuable than money. When a person is broke, time is all they've got. Time is the most beautiful thing that we can ever give another human being because we can never get the time that we spent with that person back ever again. We can always make more money, but we can never make more time."

"I learn something new from you everyday, Teacher Suzan. Thank you for the countless hours that you spend teaching me valuable lessons. I truly appreciate your time and your help, teacher. Thank you for spending your valuable time with me."

"It's my pleasure, Angelica. Trust me, the pleasure's all mine. I love volunteering and I love teaching students like you who are motivated and studious."

Teacher Suzan Nihad's Quranic Arabic roster has the whole world in the same class -- in her class, we have:
- Filipino - Canadians
- Spanish - Canadians
- Somali - Canadians
- Indian - Canadians
- Caucasian - Canadians (European-Canadians)
- Americans

CANADIAN CHARTER OF RIGHTS, FREEDOMS, & RESPONSIBILITIES

REFERENCE

MY LANGUAGE RIGHTS AS A CANADIAN:
11. EITHER ENGLISH OR FRENCH MAY BE USED IN PARLIAMENT.
12. ALL DOCUMENTS OF PARLIAMENT MUST BE PUBLISHED IN BOTH LANGUAGES.
13. MEMBERS OF THE PUBLIC CAN COMMUNICATE WITH THE FEDERAL GOVERNMENT IN EITHER LANGUAGE.
14. THE FEDERAL GOVERNMENT MUST PROVIDE SERVICES IN ENGLISH AND FRENCH.
15. EITHER LANGUAGE CAN BE USED IN COURT.

MY MINORITY LANGUAGE EDUCATION RIGHTS AS A CANADIAN:
CANADIANS HAVE A RIGHT TO HAVE THEIR CHILDREN EDUCATED IN FRENCH IF:

16. THEIR FIRST LANGUAGE IS FRENCH.
17. THEY RECEIVED THEIR OWN PRIMARY EDUCATION IN FRENCH.
18. THEY HAVE A CHILD ALREADY RECEIVING EDUCATION IN FRENCH.

ISLAMIC CLOTHING STORE
OPEN

* MRS. MARY JOE AISSA *

Last but not least, we have Mrs. Mary Joe Aissa, who is also a Muslim Filipino-Canadian. Not only is she an accountant who works for the Government of Alberta's Alberta Health Services, but she also helps a lot of families by providing them jobs through her cleaning company.

Mrs. Aissa is very generous with food, time, money, networks, resources, experience, wisdom, and knowledge. She never holds back helping other people the best way she can, whenever she can, wherever she can. She always donates her time, money, food, clothes, and hygiene packs to the needy, the poor, and the vulnerable, and she always comes up with the greatest ideas on how to fundraise money for them too, so that she's able to help more people.

We're happy, lucky, grateful, and blessed to have Mrs. Aissa in our lives. Most recently, she taught my mom how to do her own taxes. Before, my mom used to pay someone to do our taxes for us, but now, my mom can do it all on her own because Mrs. Aissa spent about 5 hours teaching and helping my mom to do it herself.

As Canadians, we must obey the law and fulfill our duties and obligations by filing our taxes. Every Canadian has a Social Insurance Number (SIN) and all Canadians are required to pay taxes so that the government can run free programs and services for the needy, the poor, and the vulnerable members of our society. It's because Canadians pay a lot of taxes that we have free healthcare, free education, and subsidized University education in Canada.

Of course, there are a lot of Canadians who are also like Mrs. Aissa who also volunteer their time to different organizations, who also donate money to countless non-profit, charitable organizations, and who also share their connections, their networks, and their resources to make our community a very vibrant place for the children, the youth, the adults, and the elderly to live in by providing free programs, services, courses/classes, and events to cater to the needs of each group.

It's thanks to people like Mrs. Aissa that our communities are much better places to live in because generous people like her give opportunities for people to have access to certain things that the needy, the poor, and the vulnerable can now also enjoy by allowing them to have equal access as the privileged people of our society.

Mrs. Aissa always says, "When we have a grateful heart, it's extremely hard NOT to treat others with respect, sincerity, genuineness, fairness, and equality that each and every single one of us deserves because everything that we do flows from our hearts."

CANADIAN CHARTER OF RIGHTS, FREEDOMS, & RESPONSIBILITIES

REFERENCE

MY CANADIAN CITIZENSHIP RESPONSIBILITIES:
19. OBEYING THE LAW:
ONE OF CANADA'S FOUNDING PRINCIPLES IS THE RULE OF LAW.
INDIVIDUALS AND GOVERNMENTS ARE REGULATED BY LAWS AND NOT BY ARBITRARY ACTIONS.
NO PERSON OR GROUP IS ABOVE THE LAW.

Aren't Canadian neighbours just so generous, thoughtful, and selfless? Honestly, where else can you find better neighbours? These are my neighbours -- this is the kind of community that we have built around ourselves. How can we ever relocate? When the community and the people in it have become our "home" where we feel safe, secure, accepted, appreciated, valued, seen, and heard.

Our skin colour is accepted. It doesn't matter that we have different skin colours.

Our language is accepted. It doesn't matter that we speak different languages.

Our religion is accepted. It doesn't matter that we have different places of worship or that my mom and I wear hijabs. Hijabs are the scarves we wear on our heads to cover our hair.

Who we are as people and how we treat others is the only thing that matters.

It's the most important thing -- the only thing.

Finally, we feel a sense of belonging where we are right now.

Finally, we feel that we have a place to call home.

Because everyone makes it their responsibility to take care of each other, to care for one another, and to ensure that everyone is cared for, that we feel that it's most definitely MORE THAN JUST coexisting and tolerating -- no, this is something completely different.

THIS IS WHAT "ACCEPTANCE" FEELS LIKE.
THIS IS WHAT "ACCEPTANCE" LOOKS LIKE.
WHEN WE ARE TREATED FAIRLY AND EQUALLY, JUST LIKE EVERYONE ELSE.
WHEN WE ARE SPOKEN TO WITH RESPECT AND DIGNITY, JUST LIKE EVERYONE ELSE.
WHEN WE ARE LOOKED AT WITHOUT JUDGMENT, JUST LIKE EVERYONE ELSE.

There is no better place that we'd rather be ... than here.

Right here. Just here. We belong here.

We've built our homes here. We've built our tribes here. We've built our lives here.

Our Canadian neighbours have become our family even if we've got different blood running through our veins. We are one. We are a family. WE ARE ALL CANADIANS.

"Nanay, how do we make sure that we treat people as an end in themselves, and NOT as a means to an end?"

"Well, by reciprocating, of course. To make sure that you don't keep on taking and taking from people, and simply be the receiver of other people's generosity, hospitality, and kindness, you simply give back to them what they give to you."

"What do you mean, Nanay?"

"I mean, you have to pay attention to people's patterns and what they give you, so you'd know exactly what to give back or how to give back. For example, Teacher Suzan loves to share her time with others, correct? She is quite generous with her time, right?"

"Yes po."

"Then, what you have to do is when you want to show her your appreciation, you also give her the gift of time."

"Could you tell me more examples po?"

"Another example is your Lola. Your Lola loves to surprise you and shower you with gifts, right?" Lola is the Tagalog term for "grandma".

"Yes po."

"So that means that you show her that you appreciate her and care for her by mirroring exactly that -- surprise her and shower her with gifts too."

"Ok, I think I understand it now. That's absolutely true, Nanay, because I believe it's better to be the giver than to be the receiver. Although, it obviously feels good to be on the receiving end too, but I just feel like it's more meaningful and purposeful to be on the giver end more."

"You really are my anak! Even your thoughts and your opinions are my carbon copy. I'm so proud of you, anak. You make me so grateful to be your mom! I'm extremely happy with the way you think. You have a beautiful soul, a beautiful mind, and a beautiful heart! You must take after me!"

"Not Abi?"

OIL
FLOUR

"Well, I guess 75% him but 100% me!"

"That doesn't even make any sense, Nanay! How does that even add up?"

"It doesn't, but I'm just stating facts!"

"Now, I think that I should cook for you to show you how much I love you, care for you, and appreciate you because that's what you do for others. You show others that you care about them by cooking delicious food for them. So, today, let me cook dinner for you and Abi, once we're done making this cake. I know how to make the best couscous and chicken adobo! I've watched you do it a million and a half times!"

"Oh, I would love that, Angelica! You are such an angel! This is exactly the reason why I named you 'Angelica' in the first place. Honestly, it's always been my wish, hope, prayer, and dream to have a personal chef in my household! Go for it! I can't wait to taste your cooking, anak!"

"Sure thing, Nanay! Anything for the best Nanay in the world!"

Angelica gave her mom a kiss on the cheek and gave her a tight hug before bolting for the kitchen, strapping on her apron, tying her hair in a ponytail, and arranging the ingredients for her couscous and chicken adobo.

Angelica is finally ready to show off her cooking prowess to her parents tonight!

'Just you wait and see! You'll definitely forget your name once you've had a taste of my cooking!' were her last thoughts before she became too preoccupied with cooking her specialty: couscous and chicken adobo.

OTHER CANADIAN RIGHTS, FREEDOMS, AND RESPONSIBILITIES

AS A CANADIAN, I ALSO ENJOY THE FOLLOWING RIGHTS & FREEDOMS:
20. FREEDOM OF PEACEFUL ASSEMBLY

21. MOBILITY RIGHTS:
CANADIANS ARE ALLOWED TO MOVE FREELY WITHIN THE COUNTRY AND THEY HAVE THE RIGHT TO ENTER AND REMAIN IN CANADA.

22. THE EQUALITY OF WOMEN AND MEN:
UNDER THE LAW, MEN AND WOMEN ARE EQUAL.
CANADA'S OPENNESS AND GENEROSITY DO NOT EXTEND TO BARBARIC CULTURAL PRACTICES THAT TOLERATE ABUSE AND GENDER-BASED VIOLENCE.
THOSE GUILTY OF THESE CRIMES ARE SEVERELY PUNISHED UNDER CANADA'S CRIMINAL LAWS.

23. LEGAL RIGHTS:
EVERYONE HAS THE RIGHT TO BE SECURE AGAINST UNREASONABLE SEARCH AND SEIZURE.

THE POLICE MUST HAVE REASONABLE GROUNDS FOR SEARCHING YOU OR YOUR HOME AND ANY EVIDENCE THAT IS UNLAWFULLY OBTAINED MAY BE EXCLUDED AT TRIAL.

EVERYONE HAS THE RIGHT NOT TO BE DETAINED OR IMPRISONED.

A PERSON MUST BE HELD IN CUSTODY ON REASONABLE GROUNDS AND MUST BE BROUGHT BEFORE A JUDGE OR JUSTICE AS SOON AS POSSIBLE OR WITHIN 24 HOURS OF DETENTION TO DECIDE IF THE DETENTION IS LAWFUL (HABEAS CORPUS).

EVERYONE HAS THE RIGHT ON ARREST OR DETENTION TO BE INFORMED PROMPTLY OF THE REASONS AND TO CONSULT COUNSEL WITHOUT DELAY AND TO BE INFORMED OF THAT RIGHT. THE POLICE USE THE CHARTER WARNING TO PROVIDE THIS INFORMATION.

EVERYONE HAS THE RIGHT TO A FAIR TRIAL WITHIN A REASONABLE TIME.

EVERYONE IS INNOCENT UNTIL PROVEN GUILTY BEYOND A REASONABLE DOUBT. CROWN COUNSEL MUST PRESENT EVIDENCE TO AN UNBIASED JUDGE OR JURY IN AN OPEN COURT TO PROVE THE ACCUSED'S GUILT. THE ACCUSED DOES NOT HAVE TO PROVE ANYTHING OR CALL ANY EVIDENCE.

EVERYONE HAS THE RIGHT TO BE TRIED BY A JUDGE AND JURY WHERE THE PUNISHMENT FOR THE OFFENCE CHARGED IS OVER 5 YEARS IMPRISONMENT. THIS PROVISION GUARANTEES THE RIGHT TO BE JUDGED BY ONE'S PEERS AND IT KEEPS OUR JUSTICE SYSTEM IN TOUCH WITH THE OPINIONS OF ORDINARY PEOPLE AND WITH CHANGING COMMUNITY STANDARDS.

EVERYONE HAS THE RIGHT NOT TO BE COMPELLED AS A WITNESS AND TO REMAIN SILENT WHEN ACCUSED OF A CRIME.

EVERYONE HAS THE RIGHT NOT TO BE SUBJECTED TO ANY CRUEL AND UNUSUAL TREATMENT OR PUNISHMENT. THE PUNISHMENT SHOULD FIT THE CRIME AND IT SHOULD MEET WITH THE BROAD PUBLIC STANDARD OF ACCEPTABILITY.

MY CANADIAN CITIZENSHIP RESPONSIBILITIES:
24. SERVING ON A JURY:
WHEN CALLED TO DO SO, YOU ARE LEGALLY REQUIRED TO SERVE.
SERVING ON A JURY IS A PRIVILEGE THAT MAKES THE JUSTICE SYSTEM WORKS AS IT DEPENDS ON IMPARTIAL JURIES MADE UP OF CITIZENS.

25. PROTECTING AND ENJOYING OUR HERITAGE AND ENVIRONMENT:
EVERY CITIZEN HAS A ROLE TO PLAY IN AVOIDING WASTE AND POLLUTION WHILE PROTECTING CANADA'S NATURAL, CULTURAL, AND ARCHITECTURAL HERITAGE FOR FUTURE GENERATIONS.

HAPPY CANADA DAY, OUR BELOVED CANADA!

Thank you to everyone who helped build this great nation. A great mosaic of different cultures, norms, people, food, religion, and languages -- a nation that we can all be proud of!

WE LOVE YOU, CANADA!

May you continue to be blessed with great leaders and mentors that the younger generation can look up to and aspire to be! Congratulations for continuously upholding and constantly honouring the Canadian Constitutions of 1867 to 1982, the Canadian Charter of Rights and Freedoms, and the Canadian Rights and Responsibilities of Citizenship.

Canadians have always been known to be kind, generous, hospitable, considerate, and polite who always smiles at everyone, who always says "please" and "thank you", and who always opens the doors for people behind them.

To the elderly and the veterans of this beautiful mosaic we call "CANADA", we would like to thank you for all of your hard work and efforts to create a Canada where everyone can feel that they belong, where everyone can feel safe and secure, and where everyone has equal opportunities to build a better future and create a better life.

THANK YOU, CANADA!

ABOUT THE AUTHOR

Chantal Magracia is a Filipino-Canadian author, educator, entrepreneur, and philanthropist, who graduated with a Bachelor of Education degree from the University of Alberta, with a major in English and a minor in Social Studies. She is an experienced teacher who has taught K-12 students, including adult learners since 2011 in Alberta, Canada.

Since elementary, she has always been extremely passionate about Character Education which encompasses values, principles, ethics, morals, virtues, good manners, right conduct, and proper etiquette. In her work, she is highly driven to model what empathy, compassion, kindness, acceptance, consideration, thoughtfulness, and understanding looks like in our daily lives. She's a dedicated and devoted life-long learner with great work ethics, who prefers to write children's books as her medium of choice, to share her learnings, reflections, epiphanies, wisdom, and growth regarding her constant pursuit of becoming the best version of herself simply by helping and uplifting others.

In 2020, she co-founded a non-profit organization known as "The Alberta Society of Islamic Fellowship" or "ASIF", and she serves as ASIF's very first President. Together with Heidi Parel, Mary Joe Aissa, Evelyn Serbout, Suzan Nihad, Mechil Templado, Maryem Ait Ali, Adila Hamad, Reem Hassen Beltaifa, and Jelena Babic, they help the poor, the needy, and the vulnerable, both locally, provincially, nationally, and internationally.

Live, Laugh, Love, and Light from Chantal V. Magracia - Ouldzini:
"THANK YOU SO MUCH FOR PURCHASING MY PASSION PROJECT!"